OUCH! THAT HURT!

LEARNING ABOUT PHYSICAL AGGRESSION

Katherine Eason

FOX EYE
PUBLISHING

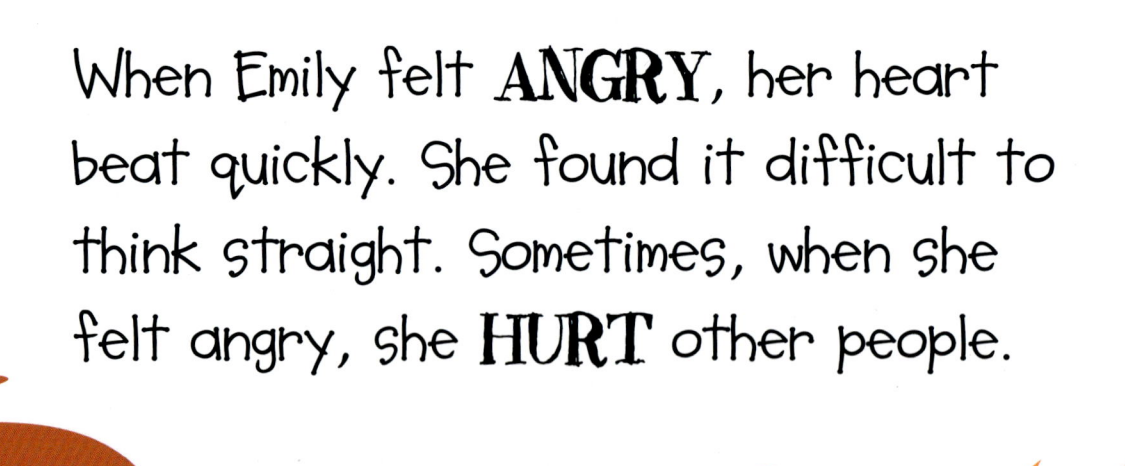

When Emily felt **ANGRY**, her heart beat quickly. She found it difficult to think straight. Sometimes, when she felt angry, she **HURT** other people.

Emily didn't know how to CALM DOWN.

One day, Emily built a den. She was very pleased with it. But then Emily's sister, Isla, knocked the den over. It was an accident. But Emily felt **ANGRY**.

She HIT Isla. Isla was HURT. She CRIED.

Emily had **TIME OUT**. Mum said to take big breaths. Emily **CALMED DOWN**. Mum said she knew Emily was angry but hitting was not OK.

Mum took the den away.

Next, Emily and Isla built towers. Isla took the last block. Emily felt **ANGRY**. She pushed Isla's tower over. Then, she **PINCHED** Isla and **PULLED** her hair.

Isla was **HURT**. She cried.

Emily had **TIME OUT** again. Mum said to count to ten. Emily **CALMED DOWN**. Mum said she knew Emily felt **ANGRY** but pinching and pulling hair were not OK.

Mum took the blocks away.

Isla took Emily's teddy. She forgot to ask first. Emily felt **ANGRY**. She **BIT** Isla. Mum took Emily's teddy away.

Mum told Emily to walk away. She **CALMED DOWN**. Mum said biting was not OK.

Mum said she knew Emily sometimes felt angry, but hurting others was not OK. How would Emily feel if someone bit her? What if they kicked her or pulled her hair? Mum said it was important to **CALM DOWN**. She asked Emily what helped her to calm down?

Emily thought about it.

The next day, Isla knocked over Emily's sandcastle. Emily felt angry. But she didn't hurt Isla. Instead, she walked away. She took deep breaths. She counted to ten. She jumped on the trampoline. Emily calmed down.

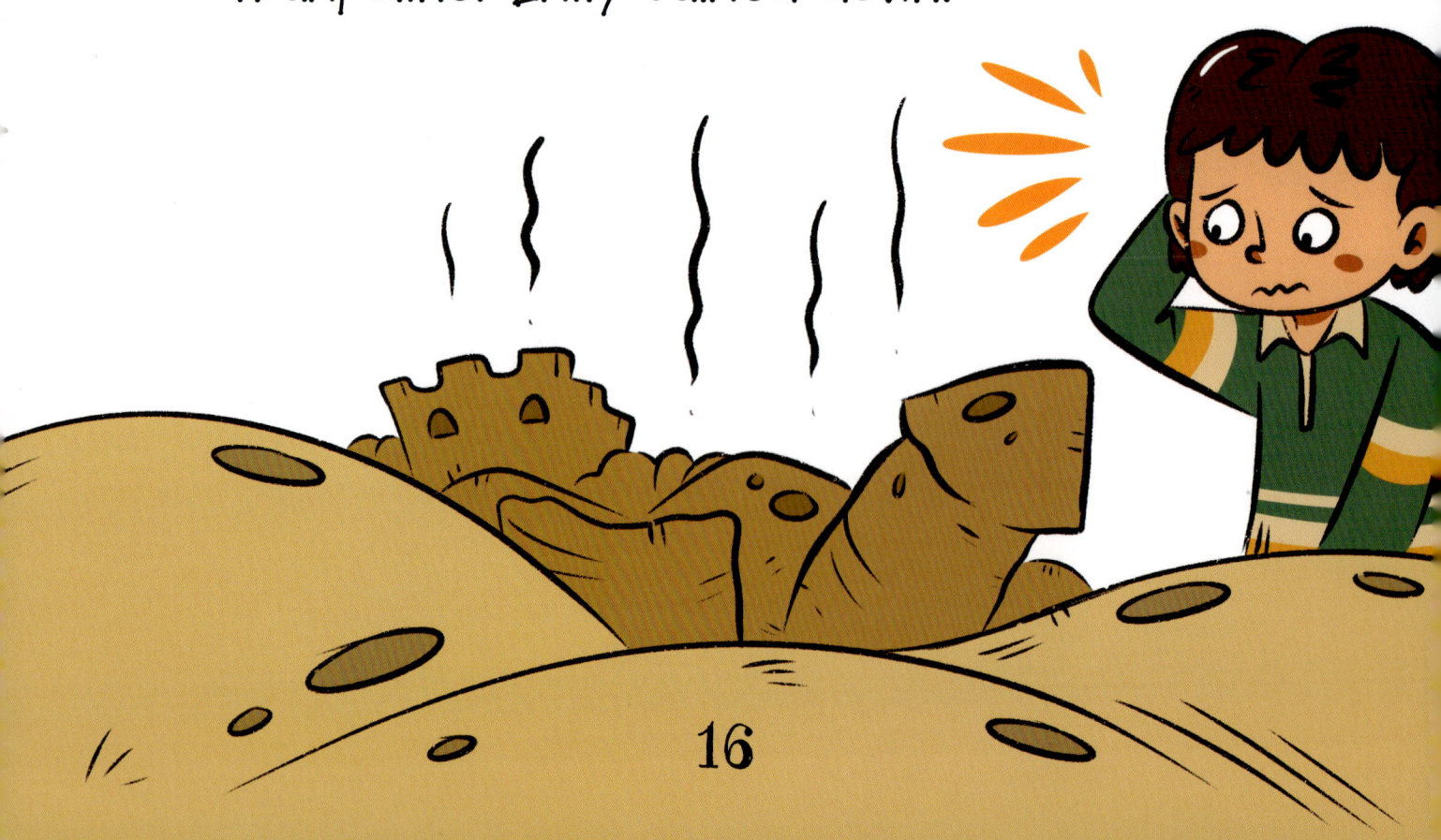

Emily felt **GOOD**. She had learnt how to **CALM DOWN**.

Words and Behaviour

Emily hurt others in this story and that caused a lot of problems.

HURT

PINCHED

PULLED

There are a lot of words to do with hurting others in this book. Can you remember all of them?

ANGRY

HIT

BIT

Let's talk about feelings and manners

This series helps children to understand difficult emotions and behaviours and how to manage them. The characters in the series have been created to show emotions and behaviours that are often seen in young children, and which can be difficult to manage.

Ouch! That Hurt!

The story in this book examines the reasons for managing anger. It looks at why calming down is important and how managing anger stops others from being hurt and feeling upset.

How to use this book

You can read this book with one child or a group of children. The book can be used to begin a discussion around complex behaviour such as physical aggression.

The book is also a reading aid, with enlarged and repeated words to help children to develop their reading skills.

How to read the story

Before beginning the story, ensure that the children you are reading to are relaxed and focused.

Take time to look at the enlarged words and the illustrations, and discuss what this book might be about before reading the story.

New words can be tricky for young children to approach. Sounding them out first, slowly and repeatedly, can help children to learn the words and become familiar with them.

How to discuss the story

When you have finished reading the story, use these questions and discussion points to examine the theme of the story with children and explore the emotions and behaviour within it:
- What do you think the story was about?
- Have you been in a situation in which you hurt someone? What was that situation?
- Do you think hurting others doesn't matter? Why?
- Do you think not hurting others is important? Why?
- What could go wrong if you hurt other people?

Titles in the series

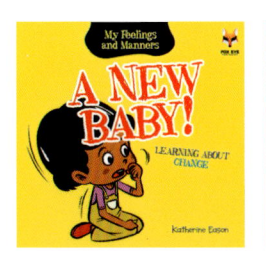

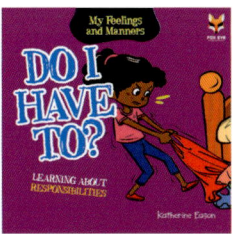

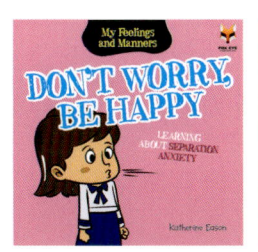

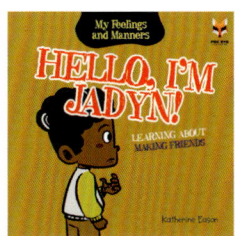

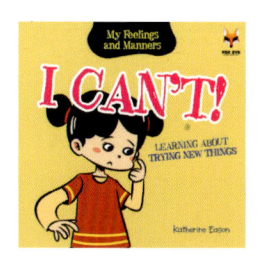

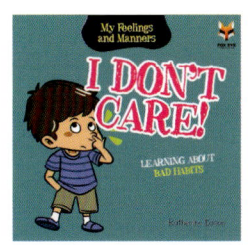

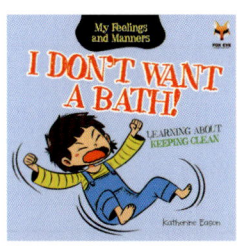

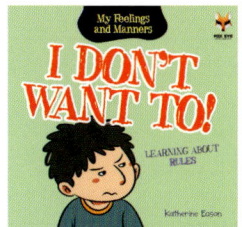

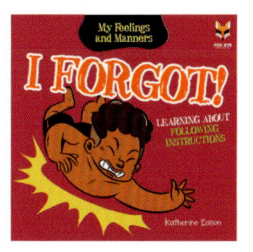

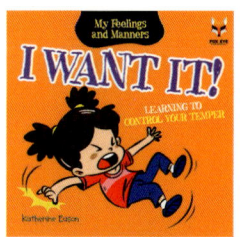

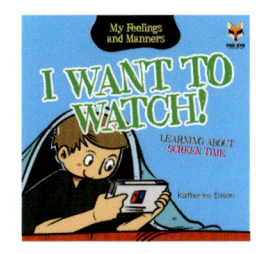

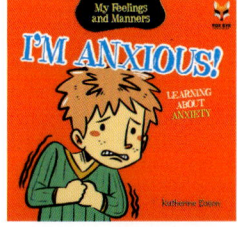

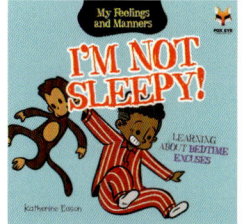

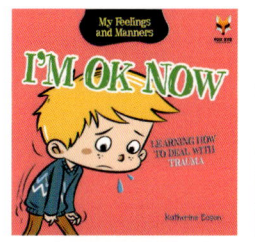

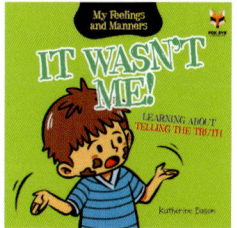

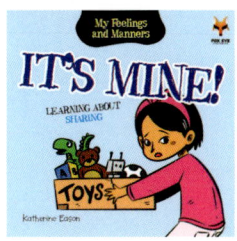

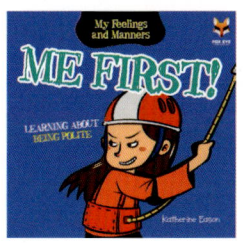

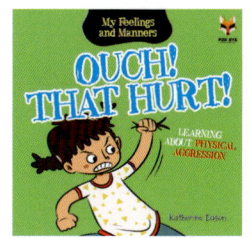

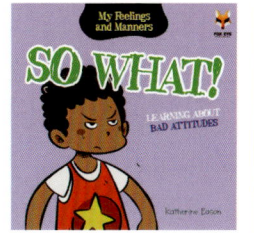

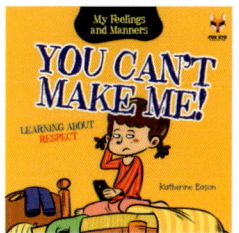

- A NEW BABY! — LEARNING ABOUT CHANGE
- DO I HAVE TO? — LEARNING ABOUT RESPONSIBILITIES
- DON'T WORRY, BE HAPPY — LEARNING ABOUT SEPARATION ANXIETY
- HELLO, I'M JADYN! — LEARNING ABOUT MAKING FRIENDS
- I CAN'T! — LEARNING ABOUT TRYING NEW THINGS
- I DON'T CARE! — LEARNING ABOUT BAD HABITS
- I DON'T WANT A BATH! — LEARNING ABOUT KEEPING CLEAN
- I DON'T WANT TO! — LEARNING ABOUT RULES
- I FORGOT! — LEARNING ABOUT FOLLOWING INSTRUCTIONS
- I WANT IT! — LEARNING TO CONTROL YOUR TEMPER
- I WANT TO WATCH! — LEARNING ABOUT SCREEN TIME
- I'M ANXIOUS! — LEARNING ABOUT ANXIETY
- I'M NOT SLEEPY! — LEARNING ABOUT BEDTIME EXCUSES
- I'M OK NOW — LEARNING HOW TO DEAL WITH TRAUMA
- IT WASN'T ME! — LEARNING ABOUT TELLING THE TRUTH
- IT'S MINE! — LEARNING ABOUT SHARING
- ME FIRST! — LEARNING ABOUT BEING POLITE
- OUCH! THAT HURT! — LEARNING ABOUT PHYSICAL AGGRESSION
- SO WHAT! — LEARNING ABOUT BAD ATTITUDES
- YOU CAN'T MAKE ME! — LEARNING ABOUT RESPECT

First published in 2023 by Fox Eye Publishing
Unit 31, Vulcan House Business Centre,
Vulcan Road, Leicester, LE5 3EF
www.foxeyepublishing.com

Copyright © 2023 Fox Eye Publishing
All rights reserved. No portion of this book may be reproduced in any form without permission from the publisher, except as permitted by U.K. copyright law.

Author: Katherine Eason
Art director: Paul Phillips
Cover designer: Emily Bailey
Editor: Jenny Rush

All illustrations by Novel

ISBN 978-1-80445-170-0

Printed in China